Parakeet Facts for Kids

Explore the Fascinating World of Budgie and Learn Everything You Need to Know About Them

Table of Contents

Introduction

Who doesn't love parakeets? They are small, colorful, and make beautiful sounds. You have probably seen their pictures and thought they would make the perfect pet for you, and you are right.

Parakeets are easy to raise, but you must know a few things before bringing your new pet home.

The book takes you into the world of parakeets, where you will discover everything about them and what makes them great pets.

Then, you will learn about their unique characteristics and features, making you love these birds even more. You will also discover the different types of parakeets so you can choose the right one for you.

You will learn how to prepare the perfect home and create a safe space for your birds to make them happy and comfortable.

Do you want to play with your new pet? Discover all the exciting toys you can buy to have fun together.

Are you ready to make the perfect meal for your birds? Learn about parakeets' diet so you can choose the right food to keep them healthy and strong.

Sometimes, birds get sick, but don't worry. The book gives tips on what to do if that happens and how to keep them healthy.

Parakeets are fascinating birds; there is so much to learn about them. You will find fun and surprising facts about their behavior and personality to understand what makes them special.

Do you want to teach your birds new tricks? Discover training and bonding techniques so you and your pet can become best friends.

Do you still have more questions about parakeets? The book answers all the questions new owners might have and gives you tips so you are fully prepared for your new birds.

Are you ready for an amazing adventure? Start reading now.

Chapter 1: Introduction

1.   Parakeets are fascinating birds. Source: https://commons.wikimedia.org/wiki/File:Gyula_Madar%C3%A1s z_-_Parakeets.jpg

If birds were singers, parakeets would be their Taylor Swift. Look at their amazing colors or listen to their beautiful melodies, and you will see why they are stars. They might even make an album with catchier songs than Harry Styles. All singers should watch out; the parakeets are coming, and they will steal your spotlight with their beautiful voices.

Parakeets are fascinating birds. This chapter gives you all the information you need to learn about them and explains why they make great pets.

Everything About the Parakeets

Did you know that parakeets and parrots are related? Both birds are native to Australia and live in large flocks or groups.

Parakeets, also known as budgies or budgerigars, are small, colorful, and friendly. They first appeared in Australia, but today, they are found in many countries around the world. However, Australia and South America are home to the largest number of parakeet species.

Parakeets don't like being alone. They are social creatures who like to be with people and other birds, playing around, exercising, and chirping. They are clever birds; you can easily train and teach tricks and commands.

You can only tell if your parakeet is male or female once they reach ten months. Female parakeets usually have a pink/brown cere, the skin around their nostril, and males have blue ceres. Sometimes, when females get older, their cheeks turn brown.

Do you know that some parakeets can talk? They can copy the sounds and words they hear from their owners. However, they will need training; not all will learn to talk. Don't be disappointed; they can still sing and make other funny sounds.

The History of Parakeets

Parakeets have been around for millions of years. Imagine these small birds flying around in ancient skies. They probably saw Egyptian workers building the pyramids or Chinese builders creating the Great Wall of China.

In 327 BC, Alexander the Great conquered India and brought many souvenirs, including parrots, to Europe. This is why the Alexandrine Parakeet was named after him.

In 367, a Greek doctor called Ctesias visited India. He saw parakeets for the first time and was awed by their beauty. However, he was surprised to hear a bird speaking Indian because he didn't know that some birds could talk. He described it as a blue-green bird with a purple face. This species is called the "Plum-headed Parakeet."

People have been raising parakeets as pets for thousands of years. In 72 A.D., in Rome, Pliny the Elder wrote one of the first books about parakeets. He described how to train these birds, care for them, and teach them to talk.

In the 1400s, parakeets left their homes in South and Central America and traveled to Europe.

Imagine yourself in ancient times before cell phones and the internet. Walking down the streets, you see a parakeet on a tree singing a beautiful melody or even speaking. How would you feel? You would be surprised, right? This was probably how people felt at the time. They might have also fallen in love with these beautiful birds right away.

Today, parakeets are one of the most popular pets in the world.

Why Parakeets Make Great Pets

How can anyone not love parakeets? They are cute, small, and friendly birds that can talk. However, there are other reasons that make parakeets the perfect pets.

Parakeets Are Intelligent

Parakeets can learn many skills, such as playing with balls, skateboarding, and standing on your hand when you call them. They are intelligent birds; you can easily train them.

They don't only listen to you because you give them treats. Parakeets love their owners and follow their commands because they share a special bond.

You can teach your bird different tricks, such as putting rings on a peg, dripping balls through hoops, counting to three, climbing ladders, or hanging upside down from your fingers.

You can also teach your bird to play hide-and-seek, peek-a-boo, and fetch. A parakeet won't be just a pet; it will be your best friend.

Parakeets Have Pretty Colors

Parakeets come in a variety of colors; each one more beautiful than the other. Some are white, others yellow, and some are a mix of yellow and green or black and gray.

Parakeets Don't Need Much

You don't need a grownup's help to take care of your birds; you can do everything yourself. Since they are small, they won't take up much space in the house or eat a lot of food.

The birds and most of their toys and accessories are cheap and you can buy them from your allowance.

Parakeets don't need much attention, so you won't feel guilty leaving them alone to go to school. Unlike dogs, they don't need to go outside for walks and won't eat your shoes or break your favorite toys.

Parakeets Can Talk

Parakeets love to talk and make noises. They can pick up a few words and repeat them, whistle, or chirp. Parakeets will still sing and make beautiful sounds even if they don't speak. You won't have a boring moment with your bird pet.

Parakeets Are Affectionate

Many people think that dogs are the only affectionate pets because they haven't met a parakeet before. Your parakeet will get excited when you return home from school, miss you and call for you when you aren't around, sit on your shoulder, and sleep next to you.

Parakeets Will Improve Your Mood

Parakeets are fun birds and playing with them will improve your mood. They can do tricks or say things that will make you laugh, they will give you affection which will make you feel calm and relaxed, and their singing will put a smile on your face.

Parakeets Don't Cause Allergies

If you are allergic to fur, you can't have dogs or cats as pets, but having a pet parakeet is safe. They won't irritate your allergies or cause any health issues.

Parakeets Increase Your Confidence

People who share a close bond with their parakeets are usually happy and have a great relationship with their family and friends. Bird owners are comfortable with their lives and confident in their abilities. The love your parakeet gives you will make you feel appreciated.

Parakeets Teach Children Responsibility

Taking care of your birds and making sure they have food and water every day will teach you responsibility and to think of others. Sweeping around their cage and cleaning after them helps you understand that pets aren't toys and should be cared for and protected.

Parakeets Make You Interesting

Most of your classmates probably have pet cats or dogs. Being the only one in class who has parakeets will make you interesting. When you meet new people, they will want to talk to you and learn more about your unique pet.

Importance of Understanding and Caring for Parakeets

Even small pets like parakeets are a big responsibility. You are bringing a living being home, so you should know how to care for them. You should learn how to feed them, what food is healthy for them and what isn't, how to prepare the perfect cage for them, and what to do when they get sick.

Learning this information is necessary to keep your bird safe. You should also understand your pet's behavior and how they normally act. This will help you notice when your bird is acting differently and try to find what's wrong.

For instance, parakeets change their voice and behavior when sick, scared, or sad. If you hear them scream, you will know this isn't normal and something must be wrong. You will act quickly to find the reason behind it and get them the help they need.

When you take care of your parakeets, they will be happy and healthy and live long lives. Remember, your pet is your best friend, so give them the love and care they deserve.

There is still more to learn about these birds; head to the next chapter to meet the parakeet.

Chapter 2: Meet the Parakeet

What is the first thing you notice about parakeets? It's probably their colors. While these birds are colorful, they have other qualities that make them special.

Parakeets' behavior is also interesting and will help you better understand their personality. Wouldn't you like to know how your pet will act when they are mad at you or jealous?

This chapter explains parakeets' physical characteristics, size, lifespan, natural habitats, behavior, and their common varieties.

Parakeets Physical Characteristics

Parakeets are colorful, small birds with a slim body and a long tail. Their small, pointed beaks aren't very long, unlike their tails, which are long like Aurora's hair.

Have you ever seen a parakeet sleeping? They usually rotate their head all the way, puff themselves up, and hide their head under their wings. They look funny and cute when they are sleeping.

There are many dangerous birds and animals in the wild that can hunt and eat parakeets. The head rotation allows them to look in different directions to search for danger so they can escape or hide if they see a predator getting close. They are clever birds, aren't they?

Colors

3. Wild parakeets are usually green with yellow feathers covered with black markings. Source: Sebastian Ritter, CC BY-SA 2.5 <https://creativecommons.org/licenses/by-sa/2.5>, via Wikimedia Commons: https://commons.wikimedia.org/wiki/File:Wellensittich02.jpg

Wild parakeets are usually green with yellow feathers covered with black markings. The back of their heads look painted with black stripes, and their tail is dark blue-green-black. Yellow-green and blue-white parakeets are the most popular. These are the ones that you will see flying around in nature.

Pet parakeets come in different colors. If you close your eyes and imagine a color combination, you will most likely find a bird like the one you pictured.

Interestingly, there aren't any red or pink parakeets because their bodies can't produce these colors. They usually get their colors from their parents.

Parakeets don't change color with age. However, if they do, there is probably something wrong with their diet. They may need more vitamins in their food. Birds who don't clean their feathers also change color, so make sure they always have access to clean water.

Most Common Parakeets Colors

- Sky blue
- Blue-black
- Gray-violet
- White
- Olive
- Light green
- Dark green
- Gray-green
- Yellow

Plumage

Parakeets' plumage or feathers also come in different colors. They can be gray, brown, black, bright yellow, green, or patterned.

Size

Parakeets weigh between 30 to 40 grams and are between 5 to 11 inches long. They are some of the smallest birds in the world.

Lifespan

Parakeets usually live between 15 to 20 years. If you take good care of your birds and feed them high-quality food, they can live a long and healthy life.

Parakeet Natural Habitat

Parakeets live as pets in people's homes in many countries around the world. In Australia, the birds' first home, wild parakeets, are often seen flying freely, coloring the country's skies like a painting.

They usually live near grass and plants so they can easily find food and stay away from wet places. Parakeets' natural habitat is in dry and hot areas, but they still like to be near water, as no living creature can survive without it.

Parakeets travel thousands of miles every year to find areas with food and water. During drought, these intelligent birds prefer to stay in less dry places, usually near the beach.

Sadly, many parakeets escape from their homes in Florida and can't find their way back. So, they come together, form flocks, and live in peace. However, some fail to survive the harsh winter.

In the U.K., wild parakeets don't usually make it through the winter because they can't handle the cold. However, many travel to warm areas in London where they can be safe and live longer.

Parakeets' favorite food is grass seeds; they usually fly for miles looking for them. They aren't picky eaters. During tough times like drought or harsh winter, they eat anything they can find, such as plants, leaves, or fruit. Parakeets can sometimes cause problems for farmers as they feed on their crops. They can be naughty little birds.

Parakeets usually lay six to eight eggs twice a year and nest in trees.

Behavior

Birds can't talk, so they can't tell you when they are sick, sad, or afraid. However, if you pay attention to their behavior and sounds, you can tell how they feel.

Head Bobbing

Parakeets head bob when they are happy. Keep watching them, and you will be in a good mood too because this behavior is very amusing. They will move their head up and down fast while making funny noises.

Parakeets bob their heads depending on their personality. Outgoing birds will move their heads and make loud noises to play around and have fun. However, a quiet bird might be shy and won't behave in a way that attracts attention.

Male parakeets usually bob their heads while singing and dancing to show they are excited and happy.

If you give them treats or show them that you enjoy watching them, they will start behaving this way to get your attention.

Wing Stretching

Parakeets enjoy stretching their wings, especially when resting for a long time. They will stretch one wing and one leg on one side and then the other, raising both wings at the same time. They won't make noises while practicing this exercise.

Head Tilting

Parakeets tilt their head or open their eyes wide when excited about something, like a new toy, or when they are feeling curious.

Scratching

Parakeets can't scratch their faces, necks, and heads. Instead, they scratch themselves using their foot, cage's bar, or a toy to scratch themselves. This usually makes them happy and relaxed.

Chewing

4. Parakeets enjoy chewing on things. Source: https://www.pexels.com/photo/green-and-red-beak-bird-on-grey-branch-97533/

Parakeets enjoy chewing on things. It is a normal behavior and nothing to worry about. Give them balsa wood or chewable toys so they can satisfy their needs.

Boredom

If your bird stands quietly on one leg, it's a sign they are bored. Play with them or get them a new toy. Parakeets who have companions don't usually become bored.

Biting

Your bird may gently bite you while holding them, this is normal behavior. However, if they are attacking you, this is a problem.

If you just got your bird, they would bite you out of fear because they still don't know you. So, take it slow.

They will bite if you play with them when they are tired and want to sleep. Your bird will also bite out of jealousy if they see you giving attention to someone else.

If they bite you while you put them back in the cage, it means they want to stay out longer and play with you.

Your bird may also bite you because they think you enjoy it. Don't pet them or give them treats when they behave this way to make it clear that this is bad behavior.

Whistling

If your bird is whistling or talking, it is healthy and happy.

Screaming

Similar to humans, screaming isn't normal behavior. Your bird is trying to tell you that it is hurt or afraid, so you must figure out what's wrong.

Wing Flapping

Your bird will flap its wings to communicate with you. This is a sign it is happy and wants your attention.

Common Varieties of Parakeets

There are different types of parakeets. Learn about them so you can choose the right bird for you.

- Plum-headed parakeet
- Brown-throated parakeet
- Olive-throated parakeet
- Orange-chinned parakeet
- Plain parakeet
- Cuban parakeet
- Monk parakeet
- Dusky-headed parakeet
- White-winged parakeet
- Lineolated parakeet (Barred Parakeet)
- Mustached parakeet
- Bourke's parakeet
- Mitered parakeet
- Alexandra's parakeet (Princess Parrot)
- Scarlet-chested parakeet
- Blue-winged parakeet
- Red Rump Parakeet
- Tui parakeet
- Yellow-chevroned parakeet
- Ringneck parakeet

- Budgerigar (Budgie)

Pay attention to your parakeet's behavior. They may be trying to tell you something. The sounds they make, their body language, and even their biting are their way of communicating their joy or pain.

Understand the meaning behind them to know your bird better.

Chapter 3: Setting Up the Perfect Parakeet Home

Everyone needs a special place to call home. It's where you feel safe, loved, and comfortable being yourself. A happy young boy, Xander feels this way about his cozy bedroom. He calls it his palace. It's his little happy place, filled with toys, books, and pictures of his favorite superheroes. He spends lots of time playing, reading, and pretending inside his lovely room.

Xander loves his home so much that he wants to create a perfect place for someone else, too – his new pet parakeet. Finally, the day arrives when Xander gets to bring home his colorful parakeet. He named his pet Donny. Watching the little bird fly around in his cage, Xander realizes he needs to make it a comfortable and happy home for his feathered friend, like his own room.

Are you ready to join Xander on this adventure? You will help him set up the perfect cage for his little bird, making sure Donny feels as safe and happy as Xander does in his own room.

Creating the Ideal Cage

5. *Picking a cage for your parakeet isn't something to rush. Source: אביתר קופל07, CC BY-SA 4.0 <https://creativecommons.org/licenses/by-sa/4.0>, via Wikimedia Commons: https://commons.wikimedia.org/wiki/File:Green_parakeet.jpg*

Taking care of the parakeet isn't just about putting them in a cage with a stick to sit on. It's more about figuring out what they like and don't like, what they need to be healthy and happy. Picking a cage for your parakeet isn't something to rush. Since they'll be spending a lot of time in their little home, you have to get one that's just right for them. It should be like their personal playground and kingdom where they rule, chirping and flying around. Here are some things you need to consider when creating the perfect cage for your parakeet:

The Cage Should Be Strong and Sturdy. Get a cage that is built to last. Flimsy cages can break easily and could even hurt your parakeet. Stainless steel cages are a great choice because they're super strong.

It Should Be Easy to Clean. You'll want a cage that's easy to wipe down and keep clean, which will help keep your parakeet healthy.

The Material Should Be Safe to Chew. Skip cages with paint. Paint can chip off; if your parakeet eats it, it could make them sick.

The Cage Should Be Accessible. Look for a cage with multiple big doors. This makes cleaning easy - you can reach all the spots inside without squeezing your hand in. Plus, you can easily add new toys and perches to keep your parakeet entertained.

It Should Have Small Bar Spacing. The space between the cage bars must be small enough so your parakeet can't wiggle out and fly away.

It Should Have Enough Wingspan (Room to Fly). Parakeets love to zip around and spread their wings. Pick a cage that's at least twice as wide as your parakeet's wingspan to keep them happy. That way, they'll have plenty of space to flap their wings freely without bumping into the sides.

Size and Space Requirements

The cage size is important because parakeets need enough space to fly around, climb, and play without feeling cramped.

For Most Parakeets: A good size is 20 inches long, 18 inches high, and 18 inches deep.

Big Birds Need Big Cages: Some parakeets, like Quakers and Indian Ringnecks, grow bigger and need more space. Get a cage that's at least 5 feet long, 3 feet deep, and 5 feet high.

Keeping More Than One: If you have a couple of parakeets, they'll need even more space. Double the size you'd get for one bird. Think of it like giving them each personal space in the cage.

Enrichment Toys and Accessories

Perches: These aren't just for sitting! They're like little gyms for your parakeet's feet. Get a bunch in different sizes and materials (think wood, rope, etc.) to keep things interesting and healthy for their toes.

Food and Water Dishes: Pick sturdy, easy-to-clean dishes that won't tip over easily. Don't put them right under perches—birdies like to keep their food and water clean!

Toys: Parakeets are smart and energetic, so they need things to keep them busy. Get them some puzzle toys, mirrors, bells, and climbing structures. Swap these out now and then to keep things fresh and exciting.

A Touch of Nature: You can add fresh branches or bird-safe plants to their cage to give your parakeet more places to perch and a little taste of the wild, which keeps them happy.

Temperature and Lighting Needs

Just the Right Temperature: Like us, parakeets like to be comfy! Aim for a temperature inside their cage between 65 and 80 degrees Fahrenheit (18 to 27 degrees Celsius for our friends who don't use Fahrenheit). Avoid drafty spots and keep the cage out of direct sunlight. Just like for us, extreme temperatures can make your feathered friend sick.

Just Enough Light: Even indoors, parakeets still need some sunshine to bask in. To mimic natural sunlight and help their bodies make vitamin D, get a special light called a full-spectrum UVB light. Turn it on for 10 to 12 hours a day. This will keep your parakeet healthy and happy.

Creating a Safe and Stimulating Environment

6. *Creating a safe and stimulating environment in your parakeet's cage is important. Source: https://commons.wikimedia.org/wiki/File:Green_parakeet.jpg*

What goes at the bottom of your parakeet's cage matters. It can affect how clean the cage stays, how it smells, and even your parakeet's feet.

Here are some good choices:

- **Newspaper.** This is popular because it's cheap, soaks up messes, and is easy to change.

- **Paper Towels or Butcher Paper.** These are good choices as well.

- **Cage Liners.** You can find these at pet stores - they're another good option.

Avoid these mistakes when setting up your parakeet's home:

Using Cat Litter, Corn Cobs, and Wood Shavings. They can make it hard for your parakeet to breathe or could be dangerous if they eat them.

Toy Overload. Don't cram the cage with toys! Even with multiple birds, too many toys can make them feel stressed. Add a few at a time and switch them out every week to keep things interesting.

Placing Them Close to Noisy Areas. While parakeets like activity, a super noisy spot can make them anxious. Put their cage in a calmer part of the room, away from the loud TV or the busy walkway.

Using Wrong Perch Materials. Not all materials are safe for perches. Avoid soft plastic toys they can chew and swallow. Skip toys with sharp hooks or tiny parts that could hurt them, too.

Loose Hanging Materials. Make sure everything hanging in the cage, like the food dish or the bath, is screwed on super tight. Loose stuff can fall and hurt your parakeet, or even worse.

No matter what you pick, make sure it's safe for your parakeet and won't hurt their health.

Chapter 4: Feeding and Nutrition

Gabriel is a kid whose eyes light up brighter than the sun whenever salad and veggies dishes appear. The boy doesn't joke with his stomach. Every mealtime is an adventure for him. He takes his precious time to enjoy everything from the first crunchy bite of his carrot to the last slice of cheese. Believe it or not, parakeets love food just as much – in their own feathery way, of course.

Just like Gabby needs a variety of healthy foods to grow big and strong, parakeets also need the right balance of nutrients to stay happy and healthy. Food keeps all living things going, from tiny ants to giant elephants. Still, getting the right food makes it even more fun.

This chapter is all about the parakeet's eating habits. You'll learn what they like to eat, how to pick the perfect food for the little guys (not just any seeds), and how much to give them at each meal. You wouldn't want your parakeet to gobble up too much food at once. It wouldn't be happy! So, get ready to learn how to create a feeding schedule and portion sizes that are just right for your feathered friend. Are you ready to learn all about parakeet nutrition?

Understanding Parakeet Diets

7. Keeping your budgie healthy is all about giving them the kind of food they can find in the wild. Source: https://www.pexels.com/photo/green-parakeet-on-tree-16049530/

Keeping your parakeet, also called a budgie, healthy is all about giving them the kind of food they can find in the wild. Remember how birds love to search for different things to eat? You can copy that by giving them a mix of tasty things. Although budgies like to try new things, it's not good for them to eat too much of one thing and not enough of another. Just like you wouldn't want to eat the same boring food every day, your budgie enjoys having different foods, too. Fruits, vegetables, and even special treats are all part of a happy bird's diet. One enjoyable snack they like is a cuttlebone – it's a bone from the sea that helps keep them strong. Seeds have too much fat, and too much of it can lead to obesity for parakeets.

What Do Parakeets Eat?

Their dinner is usually special seeds or tiny round things called pellets, made just for them. That's not all, though. They also love fresh fruits and veggies like crunchy apples, juicy carrots, leafy spinach, and even little broccoli florets. Eating a variety keeps them full of energy and gives them all the vitamins and minerals they need.

Unlike their wild friends who fly free and search for food, pet parakeets have a more relaxed life in their cages. This means they don't need to fly around as much or eat quite as much to stay healthy. In fact, too much food can make them chubby, which isn't good for them. So, you must watch what your parakeet eats, even though they'd happily gobble down all the seeds you put in their bowl. The most important thing to remember is to always keep fresh water in their cage, just like you wouldn't forget your own drink! With the right food and water, your parakeet will be chirping happily for a long time.

Choosing the Right Food

They like to eat many different things, just like you. Here's a breakdown of their birdie buffet:

Seeds: Think of seeds as tasty chips for your feathery friend. They're tasty, but too many can make them chubby. A good rule is 1.5 to 2 teaspoons a day. Also, remember seeds alone aren't enough. They need other things to grow big and strong.

Pellets: These round food things are a good option when you have little time. They fill your parakeet's tummy and keep them happy while you're away. But just like chips, they shouldn't be the only thing they eat. Pellets don't have all the vitamins and minerals your budgie needs, so offer them fresh fruits, veggies, and other treats, too.

Nuts: Walnuts, almonds, and pecans are healthy snacks with lots of good stuff. But remember, tiny bodies don't need a lot. A small piece now and then is all it takes. Avoid peanuts, though, as they can be too strong for your little friend.

Fruits and Veggies: These are super important for keeping your parakeet healthy! Think of them like colorful vitamins and minerals. Apples, bananas, and broccoli are all great choices. Wash them first and cut them up into bite-sized pieces. Fruits should only be a small part of their diet, around 5-10%.

Extra Treats: Just like you might enjoy a special cookie sometimes, your parakeet can have a treat, too. A tiny piece of fruit or a small amount of cooked oats can be a fun surprise. But remember, treats should be rare and healthy – not sugary or full of weird ingredients.

Vitamins and Minerals: They help them grow strong feathers, have shiny eyes, and be full of energy. You can get them from fresh foods, but sometimes your feathered friend might need extra help. You can talk to a vet to see if supplements are a good idea for your budgie.

Things You Should Avoid Feeding Them

What if you run out of parakeet food? Bread might seem like a good option, but it's not the best. Sandwich bread has lots of extra stuff that's not good for your feathered friend.

Here are some other foods that can be dangerous for parakeets:

- Spicy stuff like yucca.

- Mushrooms.

- Chocolate (too sweet for them).

- Green parts of tomatoes.

- Avocados.

- Raw peanuts (can make them sick).

- Uncooked beans (not good for their tummies).

- Apple seeds and pits (can cause them to choke).

- Fruits and veggies with pesticides (wash them really well first).

Even some healthy foods for people can be bad for parakeets if they have chemicals. So, always wash fruits and veggies before giving them to your little buddy.

Feeding Schedule and Portion Control

8. When parakeets eat to much food, they feel sick and not want to play. Source: Md shahanshah bappy, CC BY-SA 4.0 <https://creativecommons.org/licenses/by-sa/4.0>, via Wikimedia Commons: https://commons.wikimedia.org/wiki/File:Red-breasted_parakeet,_Satchari_National_Park.jpg

Give your parakeet the right amount of food at the right time. Too much food can make them feel sick and not want to play. It's time to learn how much and how often to feed your parakeet.

Feeding Schedule

- **Breakfast.** Give your parakeet fresh food in the morning when the sun rises. This is like how they would find food in the wild, starting their day with a meal.

- **Dinner.** Give your parakeet another meal in the early evening, before the sun sets. This will allow them to eat again before they go to sleep for the night, so they don't go to bed hungry.

- **Avoid Leaving Food Out All Day.** It might seem easy to leave food out all day for your parakeet to eat whenever they want, but it's not a good idea. Food left out for too long can go bad and grow bacteria, making your bird sick. It's better to feed your parakeet at specific times to make sure the food stays fresh and clean.

Portion Control

Understand What Your Parakeet Needs to Eat. Parakeets need a mix of different foods to stay healthy. Their diet should include seeds or pellets and fresh fruit and veggies.

Give Your Parakeet Fresh Food. Add fresh fruits and veggies to your parakeet's meals. These have vitamins and minerals that help your pet stay healthy. Apples, carrots, and leafy greens are all great choices. You can even offer a tiny piece of bell pepper for a sweet surprise. Change what you give them often, so they don't get bored. Imagine eating the same lunch every day - not fun at all.

They Don't Need to Be Overfed. Parakeets don't have tiny tummies but don't need a mountain of food either. Watch how much they eat at each meal and adjust the portion size so there's not too much left. You wouldn't want your lunch to go to waste, nor does your feathered friend.

Give Them Water to Drink. Just as you need water to stay healthy, so do parakeets! Make sure they always have a fresh bowl of clean water. It's like their personal water fountain; you should change it every day to keep it clean.

You have just unlocked the secrets of parakeet nutrition. Remember that your pet parakeet has specific needs. Offering a mix of delicious and nutritious foods like pellets, seeds, fruits, and veggies makes their bodies stay strong. Don't forget to measure how much food to give. Stick to a regular feeding schedule, and keep an eye out for those off-limits foods.

Chapter 5: Health and Wellness

10. Parakeets bring joy and happiness to many homes around the world with their colorful feathers and playful nature. Source: Vitor da Silva Gonçalves, CC BY-SA 4.0 <https://creativecommons.org/licenses/by-sa/4.0>, via Wikimedia Commons: https://commons.wikimedia.org/wiki/File:Blue_australian_parak eet.jpg

Parakeets bring joy and happiness to many homes around the world with their colorful feathers and playful nature. But just like any pet, they need proper care and attention to ensure they lead happy and healthy lives. Unfortunately, parakeets can't always tell us when they feel under the weather. They can't call a doctor or take medicine themselves. That's why they need you.

This chapter will teach you all about the parakeet's health and wellness. You'll learn about the common health problems parakeets sometimes face, from sniffles and sneezes to tummy troubles. You will also be taught how to spot a happy and healthy parakeet, so you know when everything's A-OK. It's important to take care of them every day by giving them the right food and keeping their cage clean. They also need to see the bird doctor regularly (vet) to help prevent problems before they start. Learning more about how to keep your parakeet healthy will help you take better care of them, making sure they live a long and healthy life.

Common Health Issues

Parakeets are usually strong and healthy little birds. But just like us, they can get sick too. Here are some common health problems they might face:

Avian Gastric Yeast (AGY) Infection: This is a tricky one because it's really contagious and can be tough to spot at first. Your bird might seem to be eating okay but still lose weight because AGY makes it hard to digest food properly.

Lumps and Bumps: Just like us, parakeets can get lumps growing inside them. These are called tumors and need a vet to take a look.

Swollen Neck: Sometimes, a parakeet's neck might get puffy. This could be a problem with their thyroid gland, called a goiter.

Parakeet Candidiasis: This yeast infection shows up with symptoms like being tired all the time, throwing up, and having watery droppings.

Liver Issues: Like our livers, a parakeet's liver can get sick from bad food or breathing in things they shouldn't.

Sore Feet: If your parakeet hurts their foot or their cage isn't set up right, they can get sore feet like a blister.

Parakeet Sour Crop: This happens when their crop, which is part of their digestive system, gets swollen, and the stuff inside it starts to smell sour. It is caused by certain types of yeast.

Parakeet Sneezing: If a parakeet starts sneezing or coughing, it might mean they've caught a cold or a virus that affects their nose and throat.

Vitamin Shortage: If your parakeet isn't getting enough vitamins, especially vitamin A, they can get sick.

Itchy Invaders: Tiny bugs called mites can jump on your parakeet, making them itchy and uncomfortable.

Getting Too Fat: If you give your parakeet too many treats and they don't get to fly around much, they might get chubby. This isn't healthy for them.

Birdie Flu: A sickness called Psittacosis can make your parakeet have trouble breathing and feel unwell. This can spread to people too, so seeing a vet is a must.

Stiff Joints: As parakeets get older, their joints can get stiff and sore, like arthritis in people. This can make it hard for them to move around.

If you ever see your parakeet acting a little off, like the things we talked about before (sneezing, poopy feathers, not eating), it's a good idea to take them to a special bird doctor.

These doctors are avian vets and know everything about keeping feathered friends healthy.

The sooner you take your parakeet to the vet, the easier it is to fix any problems they might have. It's the same as going to the doctor yourself – catching a cold early means you feel better faster. An avian vet can help your parakeet get back to chirping and playing happily, so don't wait if you're worried.

Signs of a Healthy Parakeet

By observing your parakeet's everyday routine, you can get a good idea of how they're feeling. Here are some signs that your pet is happy and healthy:

1. **They Poop Properly.** Healthy parakeet droppings should be like little green and black torpedoes – firm and not watery or runny. They shouldn't be any different colors, either.

2. **Their Bum-Bums Are Clean.** Underneath your parakeet's tail, where the "business" comes out, it should be clean and dry. There shouldn't be any poop stuck to their feathers.

3. **Their Breathing Doesn't Sound Funny.** A healthy parakeet won't have any sniffles or sneezes. The feathers around their nostrils (little holes by the beak) should be clean and not runny or discolored. Their breathing should be smooth and quiet, with their beak closed and their tail not bobbing up and down quickly.

4. **They Look and Feel Good.** Your parakeet's beak and nails should be a healthy length, not overgrown. Their body shouldn't have any weird lumps, bumps, or

sores. Their feathers should be smooth and pretty, not missing any patches.

5. **They Are Happy and Active.** A healthy parakeet is a curious and lively bird. They shouldn't be acting dizzy, wobbly, or having seizures. They should be excited to eat their food and treats and have a regular appetite.

6. **They Are Chatty, As Always.** Parakeets are naturally social creatures and love to chirp, sing, and even mimic sounds they hear around the house. A healthy parakeet will be vocal and engaged with their surroundings.

7. **They Are Playful.** Parakeets love to climb, swing, chew, and explore their cage. They'll often play with toys, preen their feathers, and generally be quite active. A happy parakeet will use all the fun things you provide for them in their cage.

Routine Care and Veterinary Visits

11. *You must take your parakeet to see a special bird doctor called an avian veterinarian every so often. Source: https://pixabay.com/illustrations/ai-generated-veterinary-parrot-vet-8635125/*

Imagine your parakeet could take care of you! You wouldn't want them to forget about giving you food and water sometimes, would you? Taking care of a parakeet is like a promise. It's something you do every day to keep them happy and healthy. This means cleaning their cage regularly, giving them fresh food and water, and watching out for their well-being. It might seem like a lot at first, but soon it'll be as easy as brushing your teeth.

Regular Checkups: You must take your parakeet to see a special bird doctor called an avian veterinarian every so often. These visits can help catch any health problems early before they get really serious.

Annual Visits: Grown-up parakeets should go for a checkup at least once a year. Even though parakeets can sometimes hide when they're sick, going to the vet regularly can ensure they stay healthy.

Health Check-Up: When you take your parakeet to the vet, they'll look at everything to ensure your bird is doing well. They'll check how much your bird weighs, examine their feathers and beak, and even give them shots or check for bugs.

Weighing: The vet will weigh your parakeet. Losing weight can be a sign that something's wrong with your bird.

Feather and Beak Check: The vet will also examine your parakeet's feathers and beak. It's a good sign that your parakeet is healthy if they look nice and normal.

Shots and Bug Checks: Sometimes, the vet might give your parakeet some medicine to keep them from getting sick. They might also check to see if your parakeet has any little bugs crawling on them.

First Vet Visit: If you're new to taking care of parakeets and just got your bird, it's a good idea to take them to the vet right away. The vet will make sure your new friend is healthy and give you helpful tips you might not find online.

Just like people, every parakeet is different. So, keep an eye on how they act and make changes to their care if you need to.

Keeping your parakeet healthy and happy is a rewarding experience. You can build a strong bond with your pet by understanding their common health issues, recognizing the signs of a healthy parakeet, and making sure they get the routine care they need. Remember, regular checkups with an avian veterinarian are just as necessary for your parakeet as regular visits with the doctor are for you. With a little love, care, and attention, you can ensure your parakeet lives a long and joyful life.

Chapter 6: Fun Facts and Quirky Behavior

People are interesting. We all have our funny little habits and ways of doing things that make us who we are, including you. Some people like to sing in the shower, while others love to collect weird stuff; these quirky behaviors make them fun to be around.

Just like people, parakeets have their own tricks and funny behaviors that make them awesome pets. In this part, we will explore the world of parakeets and learn all about the surprising things they do. You'll learn what makes them happy, scared, or even chatty. So, get ready to discover the secret lives of parakeets and become the best birdie buddy ever.

12. *Parakeets have fun and quirky behaviors. Source: https://www.flickr.com/photos/tambako/42438492425*

Unusual Behaviors of Parakeets

They Are Singers and Very Chatty. Parakeets are famous for mimicking sounds and even learning words! This usually means they're happy and want to chat with you. It's their way of saying "Hey friend!" Spend enough time with your parakeet and start talking to them early; they might just surprise you. Some parakeets copy your words and use them to get your attention.

They Can Scream. Loud screeches aren't happy sounds. If your parakeet is screaming, it might be scared or uncomfortable. Maybe there's a new person around, a loud noise, or something that seems scary to them.

They Pluck Their Feathers Sometimes. This can be a sign of a few things. Maybe your parakeet has allergies, itchy skin, or is bored. If they're plucking feathers a lot, take them to the vet to check things out.

They Love to Flap Their Wings. Flapping those wings could mean your parakeet wants some attention! They might be a little lonely and want you to hang out with them for a bit.

They Don't Mind Sharing Their Food. Sometimes, parakeets feed each other (and share their toys!) to show affection. It's a sweet, birdy way of saying, "I like you!".

They Bob Their Heads. If your parakeet bobs its head, it means they're happy and excited! Maybe they saw something they liked, or you gave them a yummy treat.

They Tend to Grind Their Beaks. This doesn't mean your parakeet is grumpy! Believe it or not, grinding their beak is a good sign. It means they're relaxed and getting comfy; perhaps they're getting ready for bedtime.

Parakeets Are Particular About Protecting Their Space. They can get a little possessive sometimes. Their cage is their home, and they might not like it when someone (or something) gets too close. If they puff up their feathers or act aggressively, just give them some space.

Did You Know?

13. Parakeets are lifelong lovers. Source: Marisca Kadharmestan, CC BY-SA 4.0 <https://creativecommons.org/licenses/by-sa/4.0>, via Wikimedia Commons: https://commons.wikimedia.org/wiki/File:The_Love_Birds.jpg

Parakeets Are Lifelong Lovers. They are like little birdy soulmates! Once they find a partner, they stick together for life. This is why it is recommended to get two parakeets if you want them to be happy.

Did You Know?

Parakeets Actually Have Feelings! As we said before, parakeets choose a partner for life and can get sad if their mate gets sick or dies. They might not eat much during this time. Sometimes getting them a new friend can help, but they might not always accept it right away.

Did You Know?

Parakeets Come in Different Kinds. There are 16 different types of parakeets you can keep as pets, and breeders sometimes mix them to create more colorful choices. The most common ones in America are Budgies, Lutino Budgies (bright yellow), and Opaline Budgies (pale blue with white markings).

Did You Know?

Parakeets Are Mostly Divided into Two Color Groups. Most parakeets fall into two color groups. The "blue group" has mostly blue feathers with some white, while the "green group" has green and yellow feathers.

Did You know?

Parakeets Love Taking Baths. Your parakeet likes to stay clean and enjoys taking a bath. Give them a shallow dish of lukewarm water they can splash around whenever they want. Just remember to change the water every day or two.

Did You Know?

Parakeets Have Many Names. Your parakeet's scientific name is Melopsittacus undulatus. That's a mouthful! The name Parakeet comes from the French word for "parrot." Some people also say it means "long tail."

Did You Know?

Parakeets Don't Have a Short Lifespan. They can live up to 10 years, with some reaching 15 if they're healthy and live in a calm environment. Keeping them away from drafts and loud noises helps, too.

Did You Know?

Parakeets Are Masters of Body Language. Parakeets talk with their bodies. Once you get to know your parakeet, you'll learn what it looks like when they're happy and relaxed. Watch for ruffled feathers or a wider wingspan - that might mean they're stressed or upset. They even squat a little before they poop - handy to know if you're holding them.

Unique Traits That Make Parakeets Special

1. Parakeets are very smart birds. You can teach them cool tricks like stepping onto your finger. All it takes is a little patience and reward them when they get it right.

2. Parakeets have super ears. They can hear sounds way better than humans. This helps them copy what we say and all the other noises they hear around them.

3. The more you hang out with your parakeet, the more you might notice them bringing up their swallowed food, which is how they feed their chicks, and they might do it to you if they see you as part of their family. It's a nice gesture, but too much regurgitation can mean they're getting too attached. If this happens, try giving them some space so they don't become overprotective.

4. Parakeets fall sick when their owners do. Your parakeet won't catch your cold, but they can get sick, too! They get bird versions of health problems like anemia, asthma, and even diabetes. They can also become depressed if they're lonely or don't have a cage mate.

5. A parakeet's feet can tell if they are healthy. You can actually check your parakeet's health by examining

them. Scaly feet can mean they need nutrients or might have a parasite.

6. A parakeet's beak never stops growing. To help them keep it under control, put some wooden toys and a cuttlebone in their cage. The wood helps them chew and trim their beak, and the cuttlebone gives them calcium, which is good for their bones.

So, by now, you've learned a bunch about parakeets, their funny habits, surprising facts, and all the things that make them such great pets. You might start looking at your little pal in a whole new way now. Remember, with a little love and care, you and your parakeet can be best buddies for a long time.

Chapter 7: Engaging Activities for Kids

Caring for your parakeet is the first step to bond with this fascinating bird. Did you know you can talk and play many games with them? This chapter will teach you basic tips to train them and a few bonding tricks that will make them your best friend.

You don't need to spend money on buying toys for your favorite bird; just create a few simple yet exciting DIY toys through the easy instructions mentioned here. You can also play several games with your friends and family.

14. Bonding with parakeets is really special. Source: https://www.flickr.com/photos/tgaw/14915084449

Bonding and Training Techniques

Bonding with a parakeet is almost the same as bonding with other people. Imagine you want to make a friend at school. You would approach them and talk a bit, showing your interest. You may share your lunchbox or offer to lend your school supplies. To build a friendship, you may talk to them daily until they are comfortable around you and become your friend.

That is more or less how you can bond with your parakeet.

Give your parakeet space to explore their new surroundings during the first few days.

1. Spend time near the cage and speak as if whispering to yourself. Keep your voice low and soft, and stay calm. Let them get used to you and voice slowly.

2. Offer treats like millet spray or small bits of fruit from your hand. They will see your hand as a positive experience, which can encourage them to approach you.

3. Once your parakeet is comfortable taking treats from your hand, gently try to hold them in your palm or on your finger.

4. With their wings closed, hold their body lightly, with their head between your middle and index finger. At first, only hold them for a short time, slowly increasing the time as they become used to being held.

5. Spend time with them every day, talking, whispering, offering treats, and engaging in gentle activities mentioned in the following sections.

If your parakeet is struggling after you have held them for long, place them back in their cage. They may be more independent and value their space more than your presence. Don't be disappointed because, after a day or two, they may cozy up to you again.

Remember that parakeets are social creatures. Don't leave them alone if you are going out for a few days. Don't have a second parakeet yet? Place a small mirror in their cage so they can enjoy their own company!

Training Techniques

15. Teach your parakeet to touch a stick or a fingertip with their little beak. Source: Ibrahim Husain Meraj, CC BY-SA 4.0 <https://creativecommons.org/licenses/by-sa/4.0>, via Wikimedia Commons: https://commons.wikimedia.org/wiki/File:Rose-ringed_parakeet,_Banani,_Dhaka,_July_2020_02.jpg

- **Target Training:** Teach your parakeet to touch a stick or a fingertip with their little beak. Hold the target near your parakeet and reward them with a treat when they touch it.

- **Step-Up Command:** Teach your parakeet to step onto your finger or hand on command. Gently press your finger against their belly while saying "step up" or a similar cue. Reward them with a treat when they listen. Repeat this process daily until they learn to step up.

- **Clicker Training:** Use a clicker (a device that makes a clicking sound) to applaud them when they do what you want, followed by a reward. They will learn that the sound of the clicker leads to a treat, making them more enthusiastic about performing the task.

- **Flight Recall Training:** If your parakeet is trained to fly freely in a safe indoor space, you can teach them to return to you on command. Call their name or use a specific recall cue, like "come here," while holding out a treat. When they fly back to you, reward them with a treat.

Remember that parakeets are like positive treatment. Don't punish them if they aren't learning the tricks. They may never become your friend. Use treats as rewards when they do as asked. Praise them with gentle words and a soothing tone of voice.

DIY Toys and Enrichment Ideas

Purchasing toys for your parakeet is a good idea to keep them entertained, but making the toys yourself is an even better idea to show your love.

- **Paper Roll Shredder:** Save empty toilet paper or paper towel rolls and cut them into smaller rings. Using a cotton rope, hang the rings from the top of the cage. Your parakeet will enjoy shredding the paper rings!

- **Foraging Cups:** Place small treats or seeds inside clean, empty egg carton cups or paper muffin liners. Fold the cups closed and scatter them throughout your parakeet's cage. They will have a blast foraging for the treats!

- **Bell Toys:** Attach small bells to a length of string or chain and hang them from the top of the cage. Ringing the bells with their beak or nails will be their favorite pastime!

- **Paper Bag Hideaway:** A small, clean paper bag (without handles) can become their preferred hiding spot. Place it inside the cage, open the end facing up or to the side, and watch them explore it.

- **Rope Swings:** Use a cotton rope to create a simple swing for your parakeet. Knot the ends of the rope and hang it from the top of the cage. They will perch on the rope and eventually learn to swing back and forth.

Educational Games About Parakeets

You can play these games with your friends and family so they, too, can get excited about your pet parakeet and improve your knowledge about the bird.

- **Parakeet Trivia:** Create a trivia game with questions about parakeet care, behavior, species, and interesting facts. Players can take turns answering questions and earning points for correct answers. Here are a couple of examples to get you started:

- What is the scientific name of your parakeet?

    a. Melopcactus undulactus

    b. Melopsittacus undulatus

    c. Milimeterus umbilicus

    d. Melosiraptor parakeetus

- Where are parakeets native?

    a. Austria

    b. America

    c. Australia

    d. Antarctica

- **Parakeet Bingo:** Make bingo cards with different pictures or descriptions of parakeet-related items, such as types of parakeet food, toys, behaviors, or colors. Call out descriptions, and players mark off the items on their cards. The first player to get a row or full card wins.

16. Show pictures of different parakeet species or color variations and challenge players to identify them. Source: Shamokinite, CC BY-SA 4.0 <https://creativecommons.org/licenses/by-sa/4.0>, via Wikimedia Commons: https://commons.wikimedia.org/wiki/File:Parakeet_landing-gallery1.webp

- **Parakeet Identification Game:** Show pictures of different parakeet species or color variations and challenge players to identify them. Provide information about each species or variation to help them learn more about parakeet diversity.

- **Parakeet Puzzle:** Create puzzles featuring pictures of parakeets or scenes from their natural habitat. Players can work individually or in teams to assemble the puzzles while learning about parakeet anatomy, behavior, and habitat.

Chapter 8: Frequently Asked Questions

Plenty of knowledge about parakeets is in this book, which may raise a few questions. This chapter will cover all the FAQs and give useful troubleshooting tips for new owners. The final section has interesting resources to explore to learn more about parakeets.

17. Parakeets are birds in the parrot family, also known as budgerigars or budgies. Source: https://pixabay.com/illustrations/parakeet-parrot-nature-bird-8660604/

Addressing Common Concerns

- **What Is a Parakeet?**

- Parakeets are birds in the parrot family, also known as budgerigars or budgies. Although they are small, they come in a variety of colors. They are highly social and playful, making them perfect pets.

- **What Do Parakeets Eat?**

  They eat a diet of seeds, but you can also feed them fresh fruits and vegetables. Parakeet pellets provide balanced nutrition, but you should vary their food from time to time to keep them happy.

- **How Can You Tame Your Parakeet?**

  Taming a parakeet requires patience. Spend time near the bird's cage, speak comforting words, and offer treats from your hand to build trust. After a few days, hold your hand in the cage to make the bird used to your presence before attempting to handle it.

- **How Long Do Parakeets Live?**

  With proper care, parakeets can live between 5 and 10 years, or even as long as 15 years. Their diet, environment, and genetics determine how long they'll live. It makes them just the right pets for children because they will grow with you throughout your childhood.

- **Do Parakeets Need Companionship?**

  Parakeets are social birds that depend on companionship to stay happy. While they will cherish your bond, they often prefer the company of other parakeets. Keeping at least two parakeets together is recommended so they won't be lonely and to enhance their social health.

- **How Can You Keep Your Parakeet Entertained?**

They are active and intelligent birds that like something or someone to play with. Give them bells, mirrors, swings, and chewable items. Rotating toys regularly keeps them engaged and prevents boredom.

- **Can Parakeets Talk?**

While they are capable of mimicking human speech and sounds, not all will learn to talk. Some may only copy whistles or simple phrases, while others may learn to talk very well with training and repetition.

- **How Can You Care for Your Parakeet's Health?**

Regular veterinary checkups are necessary to care for your parakeet's health. Clean their cage, provide fresh water daily, and ensure they eat a balanced diet. Watch for signs of illness, such as changes in behavior, appetite, or droppings, and contact your vet if they need help more frequently.

- **Do Parakeets Require a Specific Cage Setup?**

They need a spacious cage with horizontal bars for climbing and enough room for flying. Provide perches of different sizes and textures for their feet and include toys and other decorations. Place the cage away from direct wind and sunlight to keep them comfortable.

- **Are Parakeets Noisy Pets?**

They are quieter than larger parrot species, but they may make a range of sounds, especially in the morning and evening. Their chirping and occasional squawking are part of their natural behavior and communication. Proper training and socialization will make them less noisy.

Troubleshooting Tips for New Parakeet Owners

- **Why Is Your Parakeet Plucking Their Feathers?**

  Feather plucking isn't common, but it isn't too rare either. It may be stress, boredom, illness, or an improper diet. Check your parakeet's environment and diet. Are you switching up their food items? Do they have enough toys? If they are still plucking their feathers, talk to a veterinarian.

- **How Can You Stop Your Parakeet from Biting?**

  Biting behavior can stem from fear, territorial problems, or physical and mental discomfort. Avoid sudden movements and handle your bird gently. Use positive techniques, such as offering treats for calm behavior, and gradually make them used to handling. Avoid punishing or yelling at them, as it can make them afraid and aggressive.

- **Why Is Your Parakeet Not Eating?**

  Loss of appetite is a clear sign of illness or stress. It may also be due to a change in environment. Watch their behavior closely, make sure they have access to fresh food and water, and try offering a variety of fruits like mangoes, passion fruits, peaches, etc. If the problem persists, consult a veterinarian.

- **How Can You Train Your Parakeet to Do Tricks?**

  Be positive and patient when training your pet. Start with simple commands like step-up or targeting, and reward them with treats if they do it the right way. If they aren't able to do even the basic tricks with proper training, check for any physical health problems.

- **Why Is Your Parakeet Sleeping More Than Usual?**

  A tired parakeet might be ill, stressed, or struggling with environmental factors like extreme temperatures or bad lighting. Ensure their cage is placed in a quiet, draft-free area with enough light. Observe their behavior for any other signs of illness and consult a veterinarian if necessary.

- **How Can You Prevent Your Parakeet from Escaping Its Cage?**

  Buy a cage with a lock or a latch and account for their size. Regularly check for any loose or damaged parts that could help them escape. Consider using additional safety measures like clipping their flight feathers or using a secondary barrier, such as a mesh cover, during supervised out-of-cage time.

- **Why Is Your Parakeet Making Unusual Noises?**

  Unusual noises in parakeets can mean excitement, fear, illness, or discomfort. Check if they aren't having fun in their cage. Give them a parakeet companion or add more toys. If the behavior persists or they show other symptoms, take them to a veterinarian.

Additional Resources for Further Learning

Delve into the exciting world of parakeets with these movies and books featuring the colorful bird:

- **The Secret Life of Pets (2016):** A movie based on pets has to feature a parakeet, and Sweet Pea, the yellow and green parakeet, is one of the stars of the movie.

- **Bill and Coo (1948):** This lesser-known movie was released in the age after World War II. It shows the life of a wide variety of birds, including parakeets.

- **Budgies:** A Guide To Caring for Your Parakeet by Angela David: Know about parakeets from the other side of the world, where they are commonly known as budgies.

Conclusion

The amazing parakeet, with its bright colors and endless curiosity, can become a cherished friend, filling your life with chirps, playful antics, and a big personality.

But before you rush out and get a parakeet, remember the commitment you're making. Parakeets may seem easy to care for, but they still need a loving and responsible owner. They can live for up to a decade, so you're looking at a long-term friendship. You have also learned how to create the perfect parakeet palace, a safe and fun environment where your feathered friend can thrive. So, now you know what to do and not do when it comes to setting up the perfect home for your parakeet.

One of the most important things to keep in mind is proper nutrition. A healthy diet keeps your parakeet energized and stops them from getting sick. To ensure they stay healthy and strong, this book offers the knowledge to spot any signs of illness and give your parakeet the care it needs.

Let's not forget the fun stuff! This book also showed you the fascinating world of parakeet behavior. From their surprising intelligence to their hilarious quirks, these little birds are always amusing. Parakeets are more than just pets – they're full of funny surprises. You learned all about their silly antics and unique ways of acting and have been given a treasure trove of ideas to keep your parakeet entertained. Remember, a happy parakeet is playful, and playtime strengthens the bond between you and your feathered companion.

Finally, some common questions you might have about parakeets were also addressed. With all this information at your fingertips, you're well on your way to becoming a parakeet master. Remember, love and attention are the most important ingredients for a successful parakeet friendship. So, shower your little buddies with affection, talk to them gently, and make their environment fun. These tips will no doubt help you create a lifelong bond with your pet, filling your days with chirpy joy and unforgettable memories.

References

11 Amazing Parakeet Facts for Kids [UPDATED Facts]. (2021, August 22). Grow Kido. https://www.growkido.com/parakeet-facts-for-kids/

5 Fascinating Facts About Parakeets. (2020, June 21). Bird Street Bistro. https://www.birdstreetbistro.com/blogs/parrot-blog/5-fascinating-facts-about-parakeets

Abbott, E. (2023, October 15). Obese Parakeet: Transformative Steps for a Healthier Feathery Friend. I'm Health Fit. https://www.iamhealthfit.com/obese-parakeet/

Aldrine, L. (2021, April 16). What Do Parakeets Eat? (Complete List of Foods) (2024). Birdadviser.com. https://birdadviser.com/what-do-parakeets-eat/

All About Budgerigars. (n.d.). Petopedia. https://petopedia.petscorner.co.uk/budgies/

Books On Parakeets (19 books). (n.d.). www.goodreads.com. https://www.goodreads.com/list/show/43439.Books_On_Parakeets

Boulism. (2023, April 8). All About Parakeets: A Perfect Pet for Kids. PetHelpful. https://pethelpful.com/birds/All-About-Parakeets-A-Parents-Perspective

Budgerigars. (n.d.). Bush Heritage Australia. https://www.bushheritage.org.au/species/budgerigars

Budgie - Animal Facts for Kids - Characteristics & Pictures. (n.d.). Www.animalfunfacts.net. https://www.animalfunfacts.net/parrots/142-budgie.html

Budgie Behaviour Problems | Budgie Behaviour | Budgies | Guide | Omlet UK. (n.d.). Www.omlet.co.uk. https://www.omlet.co.uk/guide/budgies/budgie_behaviour/problems/

Budgie Colour Types | Varieties and Types | Budgies | Guide | Omlet UK. (n.d.). Www.omlet.co.uk. https://www.omlet.co.uk/guide/budgies/varieties_and_types/colours/

Budgie Parakeet Colors, Varieties, Mutations, Genetics. (2010). Puppies Are Prozac. https://puppiesareprozac.com/budgie-parakeet/colors-varieties-mutations-genetics/

Budgie Parakeet Food and Feeding Recommendations. (2010, April 13). Puppies Are Prozac. https://puppiesareprozac.com/budgie-parakeet/nutrition-food/

Burroughs, D. (2023, May 1). The Ultimate Guide on How to Take Care of a Parakeet. BirdSupplies.com. https://birdsupplies.com/blogs/news/the-ultimate-guide-on-how-to-take-care-of-a-parakeet

Clifford, G. C. (2020, July 17). What Do Parakeets Eat? (Complete Parakeet Food List). World Birds. https://worldbirds.com/what-do-parakeets-eat/

Corbett, J. (2023, December 31). 11 Fun Facts About Parakeets. Facts.net. https://facts.net/nature/animals/11-fun-facts-about-parakeets/

Cosgrove, N. (2020, June 21). 13 Types of Budgie Colors, Varieties & Mutations (With Pictures). Pet Keen. https://petkeen.com/types-of-budgies/

Cosgrove, N. (2021, July 1). How to Take Care of a Parakeet (Care Sheet & Guide 2023). Pet Keen. https://petkeen.com/how-to-take-care-of-a-parakeet/

Deering, S. (2024, January 8). Parakeet Care 101: How To Take Care of a Parakeet. BeChewy. https://be.chewy.com/5-things-you-need-to-know-about-parakeet-care/

Dhir, G. (2023, September 9). 20 Reasons Why Budgies Are Awesome Pets. Beauty of Birds. https://beautyofbirds.com/why-budgies-are-awesome-pets/

Fus, S. (2023, March 5). So, You Want to Own a Parakeet. Medium. https://medium.com/@saraafus/so-you-want-to-own-a-parakeet-a41c64559433

Gardner, K. (2012, September 28). Medical Problems in Parakeets. Pets - the Nest. https://pets.thenest.com/medical-problems-parakeets-8277.html

HappyChicken. (2022, June 21). Parakeets: Everything You Need to Know. The Happy Chicken Coop. https://www.thehappychickencoop.com/parakeets-everything-you-need-to-know/

How to Form a Bond with your Pet Bird. (2021). Kaytee.com https://www.kaytee.com/learn-care/ask-the-pet-bird-experts/how-to-bond-with-pet-bird

How to Set Up a Parakeet Cage: A Comprehensive Guide | NEURALWORD. (2023, November 19). Www.neuralword.com. https://www.neuralword.com/en/article/how-to-set-up-a-parakeet-cage-a-comprehensive-guide

Jackson, H. (2022, November 12). What Do Parakeets Eat 5 Foods In Their Diet. Paws and Claws. https://pawsandclaws.pages.dev/posts/what-do-parakeets-eat-5-foods-in-their-diet-/

Jason, A. O. (2021, August 18). Fun Parakeet Facts For Kids | Kidadl. Kidadl.com. https://kidadl.com/facts/parakeet-facts

Jay. (2023, April 28). Creating the Perfect Parakeet Habitat: Tips for Setting up a Budgie-Friendly Home. Parrot Whisper. https://parrotwhisper.com/creating-the-perfect-parakeet-habitat/

Judy. (2015, December 1). A Brief History of Parakeets | I Love Parakeets. I Love Parakeets. https://iloveparakeets.com/a-brief-history-of-parakeets/

Kingsley, B. (2022, December 22). 10 Incredible Parakeet Facts. Creature Comforts. https://creaturecomforts.pages.dev/posts/10-incredible-parakeet-facts-/

Leanne, V. (2022, December 26). Setting Up A Parakeet Cage: Your Guide To Creating The Perfect Home For Your Bird - Tame Feathers. Tamefeathers.com. https://tamefeathers.com/setting-up-a-parakeet-cage/

Leanne, V. (2023, January 10). Fascinating Facts About Parakeets For Kids: Unlock the Secrets of these Popular Pets - Tame Feathers. Tamefeathers.com. https://tamefeathers.com/facts-about-parakeets-for-kids/

Lester, J. (2023, July 13). The Ultimate Guide to Setting Up a Parakeet Cage. Www.warmlypet.com. https://www.warmlypet.com/setting-up-a-parakeet-cage/

LIBEVC. (2023, March 14). How to Train Your Parakeet & Bond With Your Pet Bird | Blog | Long Island Bird and Exotics Pet Vet. libirdexoticsvet https://www.birdexoticsvet.com/post/train-parakeets-tricks

linnearask. (2020, April 22). Five Reasons Why Parakeets Make Such Great Pets. Omlet Blog US. https://blog.omlet.us/2020/04/22/five-reasons-why-parakeets-make-such-great-pets/

Marcus, G. (2024, March 26). Best Parakeet Cage Set Up: Setting Up Your Parakeets New Home – My Pet Parakeet. MyPet Parakeet. https://mypetparakeet.com/best-parakeet-cage-set-up-setting-up-your-parakeets-new-home/

Maria Garcia, F. (2019, January 13). 5 Fascinating Fun Facts about Parakeets. My Animals. https://myanimals.com/animals/domestic-animals-animals/5-fascinating-fun-facts-about-parakeets/

Marijke. (2020, June 24). What Do Parakeets Eat? Full Parakeet Diet Guide. Psittacology. https://www.psittacology.com/what-do-parakeets-eat-full-parakeet-diet-guide/

NEER. (2023, June 26). What Do Parakeets Need in Their Cage: Essential Setup & Shopping List. Birdsdetails.com. https://birdsdetails.com/what-do-parakeets-need-in-their-cage/

Nnenna, A. (2023, August 17). Common Health Issues In Parakeets + Preventative Measures. Animajestic. https://animajestic.com/common-health-issues-in-parakeets/

Normal Budgie Behaviour | Budgie Behaviour | Budgies | Guide | Omlet UK. (n.d.). Www.omlet.co.uk.

https://www.omlet.co.uk/guide/budgies/budgie_behaviour/normal_be haviour/

Oldham, C. (2019, June 12). Budgie - Description, Habitat, Image, Diet, and Interesting Facts. Animals Network. https://animals.net/budgie/

Omlet. (2020). Parakeet Diseases | Health Problems | Parakeets | Guide | Omlet US. Www.omlet.us. https://www.omlet.us/guide/parakeets/health_problems/diseases/

Parakeet Behavior and Sounds. (2021). Kaytee.com. https://www.kaytee.com/learn-care/pet-birds/parakeet-behavior-and-sounds

Parakeets: Types, Care as Pets, Lifespan, Pictures. (n.d.). Singing-Wings-Aviary.com. https://www.singing-wings-aviary.com/parakeet

Pollock, C. (2012, January 9). Basic Information Sheet: Parakeet. LafeberVet. https://lafeber.com/vet/basic-information-sheet-for-the-parakeet/

Roy, J. (2023, August 19). DIY Parakeet Cage Set Up: 5 Steps Ultimate Guide. ParrotFoster. https://www.parrotfoster.com/parakeet-cage-set-up/

Schwarz, D. (2020, April 29). What do parakeets eat? - ExoticDirect. Exotic Direct. https://exoticdirect.co.uk/news/what-do-parakeets-eat/

Shea, L. (n.d.). Overfeeding a Parakeet / Portion Control. Lisa Shea. https://lisashea.com/petinfo/recipes/overfeeding.html

Telenko, S. (2010). The Natural Habitat of Parakeets | Cuteness. Cuteness.com. https://www.cuteness.com/article/natural-habitat-parakeets

Tips For Parakeet Care and Bonding. (2020). Kaytee.com. https://www.kaytee.com/learn-care/pet-birds/parakeet-care-and-bonding

Vallie, S. (2022, December 10). What to Know About Parakeets. WebMD. https://www.webmd.com/pets/what-to-know-about-parakeets

Wade, L. (2023, July 7). Parakeet Cere Problems - How to Prevent Them? The World's Rarest Birds. https://theworldsrarestbirds.com/parakeet-cere-problems/

What Health Problems Can Parakeets Get? A Comprehensive Guide for Pet Owners! | ThePetFAQ. (2023, May 26). ThePetFAQ. https://thepetfaq.com/what-health-problems-can-parakeets-get-a-comprehensive-guide-for-pet-owners/

Where Do Budgies Come From? | Introduction To Budgies | Budgies | Guide. (n.d.). Www.omlet.co.uk. https://www.omlet.co.uk/guide/budgies/introduction_to_budgies/natu ral_habitat/

Zayas, M. (2023, December 28). Parakeet Care Sheet. Www.petmd.com. https://www.petmd.com/bird/parakeet-care-sheet

Printed in Dunstable, United Kingdom